*Sacred Heart
Prescott*

"Let the Children Come to Me"

"Let the Children Come to Me"

A Guide for the Religious Education of Children

From Most Rev. Joseph L. Bernardin, Archbishop of Cincinnati

Imprimatur:
+ Joseph L. Bernardin
Archbishop of Cincinnati
June 22, 1976

Cover, book design and photos by Michael Reynolds.
Photos pp. 4 and 41, Anne Bingham.

SBN 0-912228-28-8

© 1976 St. Anthony Messenger Press
All rights reserved

Printed in the U.S.A.

Acknowledgments

The idea for this booklet came from Mr. and Mrs. Stanley Hater, parents of Father Robert Hater, Archdiocesan Director of Religious Education. Archbishop Joseph L. Bernardin enthusiastically backed the suggestion. The contents were developed by the staff of the Office of Religious Education. Sister Marlene Brokamp, O.S.F., was the chief author; Father Hater the general editor. The various drafts of the text were read and criticized by many parents, priests, sisters, brothers and professional religious educators, in and outside of the Archdiocese of Cincinnati. Archbishop Bernardin was personally involved in the development of the text and assumed final responsibility for it.

Contents

Introduction
    Letter from the Most Rev. Joseph L. Bernardin,
    Archbishop of Cincinnati............................. 1

Primary (ages 6-8)
    Learning Capability................................. 5
    Beliefs and Moral Teachings......................... 7
    Prayer Life of the Child........................... 13

Intermediate (ages 9-11)
    Learning Capability................................ 19
    Beliefs and Moral Teachings........................ 20
    Prayer Life of the Child........................... 25

Junior High (ages 12-14)
    Learning Capability................................ 33
    Beliefs and Moral Teachings........................ 36
    Prayer Life of the Child........................... 43

Appendix 1
    Prayers from Our Tradition......................... 47

Appendix 2
    Duties of Catholics/Precepts of the Church......... 53

Appendix 3
    Understanding of Eucharist......................... 57

Dear Friends in Christ:

Parents are their children's most important religion teachers. They teach mainly by example—by mediating the love of Jesus to their offspring. Older brothers and sisters also play an important role in teaching and motivating the young. The conclusion is clear. The family has the most direct and lasting influence on the development of a child's faith.

A faith-filled home is therefore essential if formal religious instruction is to have its best results. In such a home a child learns Christian beliefs, values and attitudes not so much by what is said as by how he or she experiences the love, mercy and forgiveness of Jesus through the everyday relationships and actions of family members.

As parents help their children grow in faith, they, too, mature and deepen their religious lives. Religious education fosters the spiritual growth of all the people of God. It helps adult Catholics continue to explore the inexhaustible riches of the Christian life.

There is a great need today for adult Catholics to appreciate more fully the riches of faith and draw more readily upon the strength it offers. Many things can help bring this about: mutual support; growth in love for God's word in the Scriptures and deeper personal understanding of Jesus' role in our lives—both of which flow from prayer; and fuller appreciation of the teaching of the Catholic Church. Family discussions and shared prayer are important ways of fostering lasting growth in faith within the family.

Religion teachers supplement, in a more formal way, the education in faith which occurs more or less informally in the home. It is important for parents and religion teachers to support and encourage each other. Their mutual trust and cooperation will help children have more and happier experiences of religion. Parent-teacher conferences help bring this about. So do family discussions about Catholic beliefs and practices. This booklet, we are hopeful, will do the same.

It is meant to help parents cooperate more consciously with the efforts being made by teachers in the formal religious instruction of their children between the ages of 6 and 14. The years before 6 are very likely more crucial in forming basic religious values, and those after 14 are vital for making Catholic values fully part of an individual's emerging personality and bringing his or her religious life to maturity. The intention here is not to minimize the importance of the years before 6 and after 14. But the booklet itself is limited to that intermediate time in a child's development which adults usually call "grade school."

Educators divide these years into three stages: the "primary" grades, ages 6 to 8; the "intermediate" grades, ages 9 to 11; and "junior high," ages 12 to 14. Each stage is considered separately here, and several things are treated in considering each.

First, how children learn. This is discussed in each section under the heading "Learning Capability." A brief description is given of what a child is able to learn at this age, together with the psychological basis for the amount and kind of religious doctrine which can be absorbed.

Second, the beliefs and moral teachings a child should be learning at home and at school. The doctrine taught at each particular age level is outlined, in order to provide a measure of the extent to which the child can be expected to understand the richness of the Christian mysteries at this stage.

Third, the prayer life of the child. The booklet describes the simple, informal ways in which a child can talk to God and grow in love for Him, and also prints many of the beautiful formal prayers which are a part of our Catholic heritage. It is not necessary that children learn all of these. They are offered as a help to parents who often ask for the texts of these prayers in order to teach them to their children.

The guidelines contained here are broad enough to cover most of the religion textbooks now available for children in parochial schools and the Confraternity of Christian Doctrine. Because of its limited purposes, the booklet does not discuss at length the development of the child's faith which takes place mainly in the home and is reinforced in church, school and other places. Instead, like formal religious education programs themselves, it presupposes a faith-filled home life.

The booklet is not only intended for parents and teachers—it is dedicated to them. Theirs is a great and beautiful vocation: to form a new generation of loving, informed and committed followers of the Lord Jesus. I pray that this publication will assist them in fulfilling this noble task.

Asking God's blessing upon all who may read and use this booklet, I am

Sincerely yours in Christ,

+ Joseph L. Bernardin

Most Rev. Joseph L. Bernardin
Archbishop of Cincinnati

PRIMARY (Ages 6 - 8)

LEARNING CAPABILITY

Formative Years

Six- to eight-year-olds have very absorbent minds. Because they are so impressionable, much of the groundwork for their later, fuller acceptance of the Catholic heritage is laid at this stage.

Concrete Approach

These children feel, think of and imagine themselves to be the center of all things. They are very concrete; they understand things just as they see or hear them. Unlike adults, they are not able to think in abstract concepts. Instead they dwell in an inner world of fantasy, full of lively images and vivid color.

Attitudes

At this age children are forming attitudes. They have a strong desire to imitate, are very active, have a short attention span, are surprised at many things — and full of surprises themselves, and are very curious. Younger children, those aged 6 and 7,

consider themselves good or bad on the basis of adult approval or disapproval. As they grow older, they begin to develop their own sense of fair play, justice and responsibility.

Religious Response

Children at this stage are able to respond readily and reverently to God's love as they learn about Jesus in songs, drama, pictures and formal and informal prayer. Gradually they move from seeing themselves simply as individuals to thinking of themselves as members of a group or community. This is an ideal time for them to acquire basic principles of moral knowledge and develop habits based on this knowledge. Conscience formation and character training should be approached positively. Children should be taught to have a sense of self-worth, because a good attitude toward oneself is a foundation for love of God and neighbor. They should learn how to please our Heavenly Father in their daily acts.

Language

Because of exposure to television and radio as well as older children and adults, primary grade children often use words they do not fully understand. The vocabulary which they can use readily and with full comprehension is really quite limited. They should therefore be addressed in simple, concrete language.

Qualities

A sense of awe, love of mystery, delight in ritual, reverence for all that has life, trust, spontaneity, openness to love and a need to be loved are natural, positive qualities of these children. Religious education should nurture these qualities. They make the child at this age a special delight.

BELIEFS AND MORAL TEACHINGS

Trinity

Primary age children should be led gently to meet and live on familiar terms with the Father, Son and Holy Spirit. They find it easy to meet Jesus, the God-man. Through Him they are in turn introduced to His Father, who gives life, and to the Spirit, who expresses the love between Father and Son.

Father

Children are delighted by the wondrousness of the gifts of their Father-Creator. They should learn about all that God has made — angels, people, nature and the universe — and see these works of creation as expressions of God's love and signs of His presence. They learn that God created each of them individually in order to know, love and serve Him and live with Him forever.

Grace and Baptism

At this time children are introduced to the meaning of grace as God's life and love and to the meaning of

Baptism. They learn that through Baptism all are meant to live as members of God's family and to share together the gifts of His life and love.

Jesus

Children of this age can be helped to understand the mysteries of the Incarnation and Redemption by explanations in terms like these: "God the Father loves and cares for people so much that He sent His Son, Jesus, to us. Jesus came to save us from sin and lead all people back to the Father. He did this by His teaching and by dying on the cross and rising on Easter Sunday. Jesus teaches us to love one another. He was willing to die rather than desert His friends or disobey His Father. In Baptism, the Risen Jesus makes each of us a child of God and gives us faith, hope and love."

The Spirit

In explaining Baptism, one also has an opportunity to teach children about the Holy Spirit, who comes to us in this sacrament. Jesus continues to act in the world today through the Spirit.

Sacraments

The sacraments should be presented as outward signs and causes of God's grace. They are special signs of Jesus' presence and action in the world today. They are the principal actions through which Jesus gives His Spirit to Christians and makes them a holy people, and they are themselves encounters with the Lord. Much of religious education at the primary level is concerned in a special way with the sacraments of the Eucharist and Penance.

Eucharist

The explanation about the Eucharist given to children of any age takes place within the context of our understanding of the Eucharist as both a sacred "meal" and a "sacrifice." The Mass is a memorial meal at which we remember and make present the saving death and resurrection of Jesus Christ, His once and for all sacrifice to the Father.

Children of this age respond well to the idea that,

in the Eucharist, Jesus invites them to join Him in offering themselves to the Father during the family meal of God's special friends and children. The members of God's family, the Christian community, gather together in the parish church for this holy meal which we call the Mass. At the Eucharist the people recall what Jesus did the night before He died and when He offered Himself on the cross to the Father. And Jesus Himself is present to renew these actions of His. The people offer themselves to God when the priest offers the bread and wine. Jesus offers Himself to us as the Bread of Life in Holy Communion. Each person says "Amen" when the priest says "The Body of Christ" in order to proclaim his or her belief that what was bread is now Jesus (cf. Appendix 3).

Morality

At this age children are also introduced to the concepts of sin, sorrow and God's love and forgiveness. This is done according to their ability to understand these realities. For example: "God made all things and persons good, but sometimes people do not use things or do things as God wants. They go against God and do what they know is wrong. Sometimes this is so bad that the love of God leaves their hearts. At other times it is not that bad, but God still does not want such things to be done. But God will always forgive us if we are sorry." Children should have opportunities to witness and experience forgiveness — parents forgiving each other, parents forgiving children, children forgiving parents and brothers and sisters. In this way they learn to understand and accept God's loving forgiveness. Formation of conscience is a delicate matter. Although sin is a reality in everyone's life, it presupposes deliberation, choice and malice. Children should not be loaded down with guilt or made to think that they are capable of a degree of malice of which they are really incapable.

Penance

It is the mind of the Holy See that the sacrament of

Penance be celebrated before the reception of first Eucharist. There are many options in the sacrament of Penance. It may be received in the confessional or directly facing the priest. Here are some suggestions for guiding children's private confession.

1. Before confession ask for Jesus' help. Tell Him how much you love Him, try to remember anything you did wrong and why you did it, and ask Jesus to forgive you and help you be better.

2. When your time comes to enter the confessional or approach the priest, kneel or sit where you can see him. Wait for him to speak to you.

3. Make the Sign of the Cross and listen to the priest as he prays for you. Answer "Amen."

4. Listen to the Word of God.

5. Tell the priest the things you are sorry for.

6. Listen to the priest's advice and what he tells you to do for your penance.

7. When the priest asks you to tell Jesus you are sorry, say a sincere Act of Contrition. (There is no one approved form. Several are given in the renewed rite of Penance, including the two given below. These or any suitable prayer for forgiveness may be used.)

Examples

FATHER, I have sinned against you and I am not worthy to be called your son. Be merciful to me, a sinner (Luke 15:18; 18:13).

LORD, Jesus, Son of God, have mercy on me, a sinner (Jesus Prayer).

8. Listen to the priest's prayer of forgiveness and absolution. Answer "Amen."

9. The priest then says "Give thanks to the Lord for He is good." Answer "His mercy endures forever."

10. The priest will then dismiss you, saying words like "The Lord has freed you from your sins. Go in Peace."

11. Return to your place. Do whatever the priest has told you to do for your penance, such as saying certain prayers or performing certain good acts.

Church

Besides the sacraments, another special sign of Jesus' presence in the world is His Church. As members of the Church all Catholics are to work for the coming of the Father's kingdom by living Christian lives, loving God and neighbor. Practicing the virtues is one way of expressing Catholic values and experiencing the Kingdom of God here on earth.

Mary Mary is the Mother of Jesus. Since we are God's children and Jesus' brothers and sisters, she is also our mother. Mary always said "yes" to God — she always accepted His will for her. Religious education tries to help children see Mary not only as singularly blessed, but also as having a real role and meaning for their lives and needs. This meaning is that, apart from God Himself, she is our closest friend in heaven. Parents and teachers should explain the special place of the Virgin Mary in God's plan of salvation and in the Church.

PRAYER LIFE

Liturgical Prayer The members of the Christian community are called to participate in the formal liturgical prayer of the Church. Children of primary age should be in-

volved in the Church's liturgy, according to their ability to understand and appreciate what is happening. Liturgical prayer is the highest form of prayer. It is the official prayer of the Church. Through it we learn that we are blessed by God's love in Jesus Christ, so that we can respond in turn to His love by Christian service to God and neighbor. Liturgical prayer centers upon Jesus, His prayer and saving activity, continued in and by the Church. Its purpose is both the worship of God and the salvation of human beings.

The Mass is the Church's "great prayer." Children understand the Mass as an act of God's family — a special gathering where Christ becomes present among us under the appearance of bread and wine.

As the child learns to read, parents should help him or her follow the common Mass responses as found in the hymnal or missalettes. Repetition makes it easy to learn the correct liturgical responses, acclamations, gestures and postures used at Mass. Visits to the Baptismal font with appropriate prayers are encouraged. So are communal penance services. Children should be allowed to examine closely the objects used in worship to honor God: holy water, candles, incense, vestments, sacred vessels, etc. This will help them develop a deeper appreciation of sacramental celebrations and prayer, in which material things are used to worship God.

Spontaneous Prayer

Children should also be taught to pray simply, by talking to God as to a friend and saying what is in their hearts. They should learn to listen for God's answer. This is called spontaneous prayer. It is something that can happen often during the day. Spontaneous prayers of love, sorrow, thanksgiving, awe, wonder and trust are important parts of the child's life of prayer. Morning and night prayers and short visits to the Blessed Sacrament should be encouraged. Prayers at meals are important daily opportunities for family members to share their prayer life. Parents can help their children pray spontaneously by encouraging them to be aware of the beauty and goodness around them — beauty and goodness which reflect God Himself. Their prayer then becomes a natural response to what they see and experience. For example:

> Dear God, I love Your world.
> Thank You for making it so beautiful for me.
> Amen.

> Thank You, God, for making night and day with time for sleep and time for play. Amen.

Other Forms of Prayer

Silence is an important part of prayer. Children should be taught to listen silently as God speaks to them and to experience God's interior presence in silence. Prayer can also happen in songs and celebrations. Introduce God's word to the child at an early age with short, simple readings from the Bible—for example, the stories of Christmas, the Last Supper and Easter. Special children's translations of the Bible should be used when appropriate. It is also good to share with children words of peace and joy from the Bible, as well as accounts of doing good. Readings from the Psalms can deepen a child's life of prayer.

Children should also experience sacred music, which adds another dimension of beauty to prayer and is a form of prayer itself. It is very appropriate that children be introduced to contemporary musical forms, but they should also have the opportunity to learn the traditional hymns of the Catholic heritage.

Formal Prayer

Children need to learn how to pray together in community. Therefore they should learn certain prayers which are commonly said by the Christian community. These include the Sign of the Cross, the Our Father, the Hail Mary, and the Glory Be to the Father.

Sign of the Cross

In the name of the Father, and of the Son, and of the Holy Spirit. Amen.

Our Father

Our Father who art in heaven, hallowed be Thy name; Thy kingdom come; Thy will be done on earth as it is in heaven. Give us this day our daily bread; and forgive us our trespasses as we forgive those who trespass against us; and lead us not into temptation, but deliver us from evil. Amen.

Hail Mary

Hail Mary, full of grace! the Lord is with thee; blessed art thou among women, and blessed is the fruit of thy womb, Jesus. Holy Mary, Mother of God, pray for us sinners, now and at the hour of our death. Amen.

Glory Be to the Father

Glory be to the Father, and to the Son, and to the Holy Spirit. As it was in the beginning, is now, and ever shall be, world without end. Amen.

Angel of God

Angel of God, my guardian dear,
To whom God's love commits me here;
Ever this day be at my side,
To light and guard,
To rule and guide. Amen.

INTERMEDIATE (Ages 9-11)

LEARNING CAPABILITY

Characteristics   In the "intermediate" grade years, children are exploring life through a wide range of interests. This is an age of independence and curiosity. More capable of self-discipline than before, children at this time tend to be legalistic, literal and exact. They have a strong sense of fair play. They are developing an ability to conceptualize and to see the connection between causes and effects. They want to know "why" and find simple answers helpful.

Community   At this age children are very sensitive to the judgments and standards of their peers. They want to belong to the "group" and also seek special friends. They are interested in people and want heroes and models for imitation.

Qualities	Children in these years acquire a more sophisticated awareness of time, and it is now possible to help them develop a sense of history. Their need and ability to "belong" are expanding beyond the family. They are intrigued by what they find mysterious. They appreciate loyalty and honesty, and enjoy group activity. They need to feel that they are successful in communicating to their parents their growing concern with matters outside the family, and they also need to feel that they are a part of family discussions. It is important to continue to foster their growing sense of self-worth.
Religious Response	These children appreciate the order they find in creation and in the Church. They relate to God as an all-loving Father and to Jesus as a personal leader of great courage. They are responsive to Gospel stories portraying Jesus as a hero to be imitated.

BELIEFS AND MORAL TEACHINGS

Trinity	Religious instruction in the intermediate grades aims at helping children realize that the three Persons of the Trinity are uniquely and deeply involved with the human race. The work of the Father is presented as creation, the work of the Son as salvation, and the work of the Holy Spirit as sanctification.
Christ	Christ is seen especially as the one who fulfilled the promise of a Redeemer, as the great Reconciler who leads each of us personally to the Father. At this time children become more fully acquainted with the mystery of God become Man through the Incarnation and of Jesus' death as the instrument of our redemption, and with the value of sacrifice and suffering as important elements of a Christian life modeled on the life of Jesus.
Sacraments	Further growth in understanding of the sacraments — Baptism, Confirmation, the Eucharist, Penance,

Anointing of the Sick, Holy Orders and Matrimony—can take place at this age. So can a deeper experience of the Church as a worshipping community. Children begin to appreciate the differences in the liturgical seasons of the year and to recognize the different themes in worship.

Morality

A more formal introduction to morality is necessary now. Children should be helped to understand that God has established norms for our action as brothers and sisters of Jesus. Examples help them decide whether their actions are right or wrong—that is, whether they are or are not what God wants them to do. The Commandments are presented and taught as expressions of moral principles; by observing them we are responding lovingly and obediently to God's goodness.

At this time children are taught that Christ announced a new law which went beyond even the Old Testament commandments. This law teaches us that Christian life must be patterned on the life of Christ.

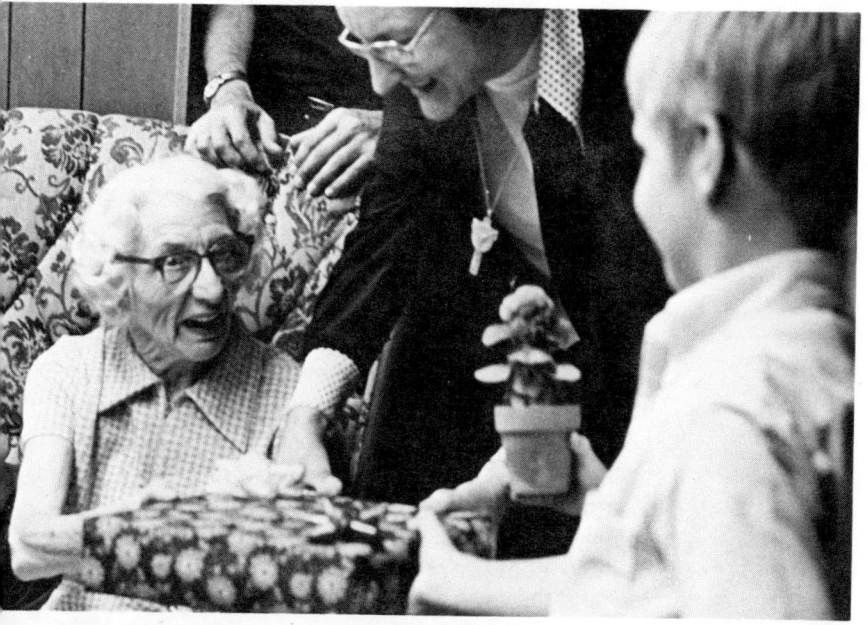

It must be a life of generous concern and self-giving for others, a life entirely in union with the Father's will, a life of total and unselfish love.

Through the Ten Commandments, Jesus' law of love and the teachings of the Church, the child learns that right and wrong involve personal decisions of the kind mentioned above. He or she is led to see the consequences and responsibilities that accompany each decision.

During these years children are growing in an awareness of sexuality. A positive environment should be created at home and in school, so that children can appreciate sexuality as good and normal, and be given proper sexual instruction. All sexual education should rest on the premise that chastity and purity are important and desirable Christian virtues.

God's Commandments

1. I, the Lord, am your God. You shall not have other gods besides me.
2. You shall not take the name of the Lord, your God, in vain.
3. Remember to keep holy the sabbath day.
4. Honor your father and mother.
5. You shall not kill.
6. You shall not commit adultery.
7. You shall not steal.
8. You shall not bear false witness against your neighbor.
9. You shall not covet your neighbor's wife.
10. You shall not covet anything that belongs to your neighbor.

Jesus' Law of Love

Jesus said: "You shall love the Lord your God with your whole heart, with your whole soul, and with all your mind. This is the greatest and first commandment. The second is like it: You shall love your neighbor as yourself. On these two commandments the whole law is based, and the prophets as well." (Matthew 22: 37-40)

Church

The Church, as the family of God, helps the intermediate-age child know God's will more perfectly through the assistance of parents, teachers, priests and other adults.

At this time children examine the lives of some of the Old Testament's greatest men and women. They discover that God's chosen people had to struggle with the same kind of questions Christians face today — and grew by responding courageously. Children also learn that in the Gospels Jesus teaches us how to live and helps us answer our questions about life, suffering, death, judgment, heaven, purgatory, and hell.

Social Justice

Now, too, children are helped to integrate aspects of the values of justice and peace into their experience of learning and living. They are encouraged to grasp the meaning of the fact that Catholics have a moral responsibility to contribute to a more just and peaceful society for all people.

Ecumenism

These children are also encouraged to respect the beliefs of other religious, ethnic and racial groups. Although the fact that different people believe different things does not mean that all beliefs are equally valid and true, children should learn to adopt a positive attitude toward people who are sincere in their convictions and an appreciation of the elements of goodness and truth in their beliefs.

PRAYER LIFE

Liturgical Prayer

Religious services shared as a community which are not part of the formal liturgical life of the Church (that is the Mass, the other sacraments and the Divine Office) are called "para-liturgical." Using Psalms, Scripture readings and song, such celebrations may be centered upon the liturgical seasons and their feasts in order to deepen experience of the Church's liturgical prayer. Para-liturgical services are an important part of the prayer life of children at this age. Benediction and exposition of the Blessed Sacrament should be explained to help foster belief in the Real Presence and the desire to receive Communion.

They should be taught and helped to compose their own simple para-liturgical services to share with others. A simple format is best: an opening song, a reading from Scripture, a Psalm response, shared reflections on the reading, and a closing song. This is an ideal time to teach children about Jesus, Mary and the saints. Children should also have opportunities to share their thoughts and feelings through prayer. Prayer of this kind is excellent for families. The children can take turns composing para-liturgical services for special family occasions — birthdays, wedding anniversaries, Advent celebrations, and so on.

The cycle of the Church Year, with its many different feasts and themes, is very rich.

Advent Season: We recall the longing of Isaiah the Prophet, the penance of John the Baptizer, the prayer of Mary, all of which help us prepare for Christ's coming. Traditions include the Advent wreath, the Jesse tree, and the Mary candle. During the Advent season a notable Marian feast that occurs is the Immaculate Conception, December 8.

Christmas Season: We celebrate God's coming to

us as a man in order to take us to Himself. Traditions include the Christmas tree and crib, the Christmas candle, and Twelfth Night celebrations.

Time after Christmas: Among the feasts and observances are the Solemnity of Mary (January 1), the "Chair of Unity" Octave (January 18-25), Candlemas Day (February 2), and the Feast of the Presentation of Our Lord (called the Feast of Light).

Lenten Season: During Lent we reflect on the significance of Baptism, besides fostering a spirit of penance in preparation for celebrating the paschal mystery (that is, the life, death and resurrection of Jesus). Traditions include the blessing of ashes on Ash Wednesday, doing without some things as a personal offering, the Stations of the Cross, the rites of Palm Sunday, Holy Thursday and Good Friday.

Easter Season: Christ's triumph over death is celebrated with great joy, using symbols of abundant life and of beauty and goodness. Traditions symbolic of these themes include lilies, Easter eggs and rabbits. Pentecost, the feast of the Spirit, who wishes to inflame our hearts with divine love, concludes the Easter Season.

Ordinary Time of the Year: During this season we celebrate such other feasts as Trinity Sunday, Corpus Christi (the Feast of the Body and Blood of Christ), the Assumption (August 15), Mary's birthday (September 8), All Saints (November 1), and Christ the King.

Spontaneous Prayer

The child's private prayer life, including morning and evening prayers, should grow during these middle years. Children may be encouraged to share their prayers with others. Appropriate themes for prayer include petitions for faith, hope and love; concern for the well being of others; prayers of mercy, praise, thanksgiving, sorrow; the need for guidance in

knowing the right thing to do and the courage to do it; strength to live as Christ lived.

It is also important that parents share their prayer life with their children. Thus children have a model for prayer and are also reminded that, ideally, prayer arises spontaneously and naturally during the day of a person who is living close to God.

There is no one "set" formula for an Act of Faith, Hope or Love. Here, however, are suggested forms. (Note that children should be encouraged to compose their own.)

Act of Faith

Oh God, I want to be Your child.
I want You to be my Father.
I believe in You! I love You!

Jesus, I believe You are alive!
Come to me and share Your love with me.

Act of Hope

Jesus, You can do all things.
I will always trust You.
You are always near me.

Act of Love

O God, I love You above all people and things because You are all good. I love my neighbor as myself for love of You.

Meditation Children in the intermediate grades should be taught to appreciate silence because it is necessary for prayer — because, indeed, given the proper dispositions, it is a kind of prayer in itself. It is very important that the child have time for reflection and meditation, even though these may be on a very simple level.

Formal Prayers It is also important that the child review the simple formal prayers which were learned in the primary grades and learn to say them with a fresh appreciation for their beauty and meaning. Other formal prayers and formulas which are a rich part of the Catholic tradition may be learned as well. The Nicene Creed is the formula used in Mass. Here is the approved new translation of the Apostles' Creed, which can be used in Masses for children.

Apostles' Creed

I believe in God, the Father almighty, creator of heaven and earth. I believe in Jesus Christ, His only Son, our Lord. He was conceived by the power of the Holy Spirit and born of the Virgin Mary. He suffered under Pontius Pilate, was crucified, died, and was buried. He descended to the dead. On the third day He rose again. He ascended into heaven, and is seated at the right hand of the Father. He will come again to judge

the living and the dead.
I believe in the Holy Spirit, the holy catholic Church, the communion of saints, the forgiveness of sins, the resurrection of the body, and the life everlasting.

                                    Amen.

The Rosary and Its Mysteries

The Rosary can be said either as a communal or a private prayer. It calls to mind the five joyful, five sorrowful and five glorious mysteries in the lives of Christ and His Blessed Mother. It is composed of fifteen decades, each consisting of one Our Father, ten Hail Marys, and one Gloria.

The Apostles' Creed is said on the Crucifix; the Our Father is said on each of the large beads; the Hail Mary on each of the small beads; the Gloria after the three Hail Marys at the beginning of the Rosary, and after each group of small beads.

Joyful Mysteries

The Annunciation
The Visitation
The Birth of Christ
The Presentation of Jesus in the Temple
The Finding of Jesus in the Temple

Sorrowful Mysteries

The Agony in the Garden
The Scourging at the Pillar
The Crowning with Thorns
The Carrying of the Cross
The Crucifixion

Glorious Mysteries

The Resurrection
The Ascension
The Descent of the Holy Spirit
The Assumption of Mary into Heaven
The Coronation of Mary as Queen of Heaven and Earth

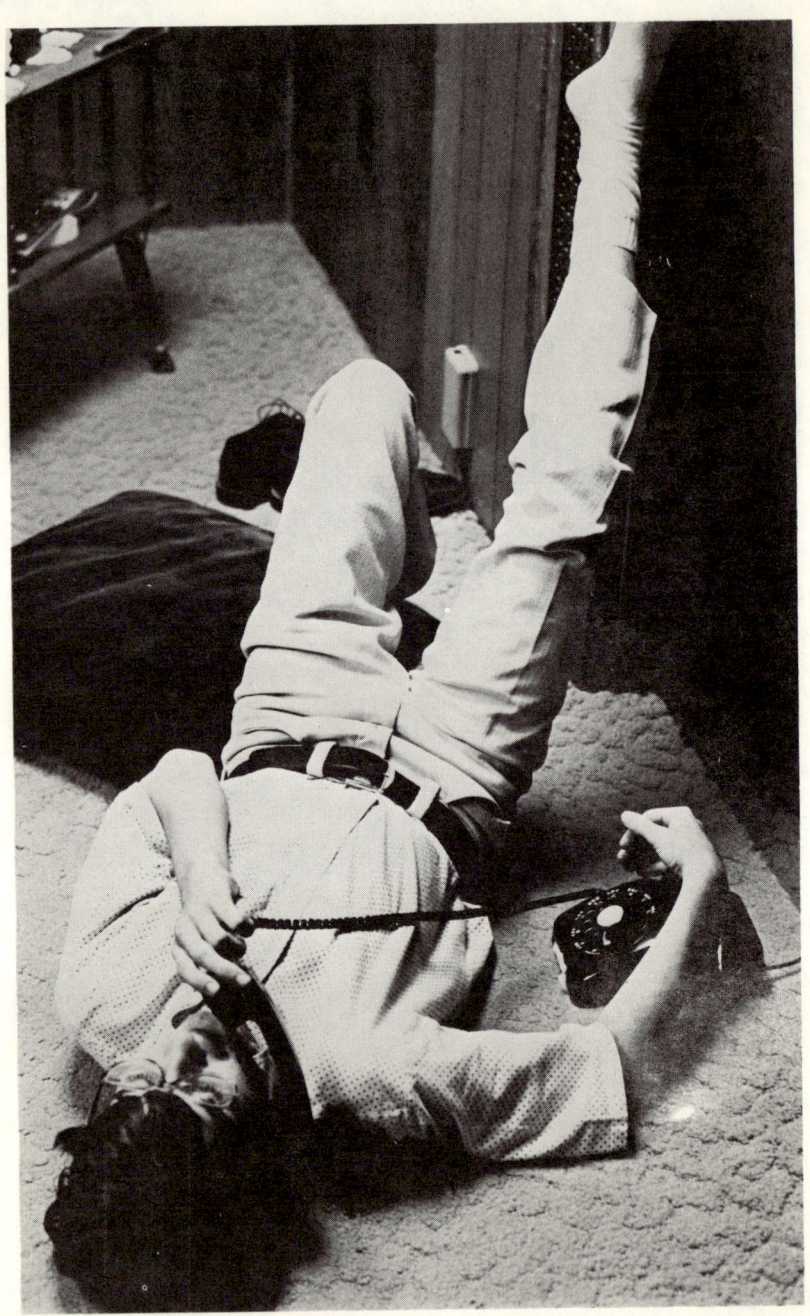

JUNIOR HIGH (Ages 12 - 14)

LEARNING CAPABILITY

Adolescence — Junior high school students can be a source of bewilderment to parents and themselves. In Western culture adolescence is a long period, marked by growth and change in almost every part of the young person's life.

Challenge — The emotional challenges to the adolescent are great. At this time youngsters are beginning to seek independence and discover their own individual personalities and identities, separate from their parents' protective concern. This is a time of testing and experimentation, faltering poise, self-consciousness, conflict and insecurity. It is also a time when young people must cope with their emerging sexuality and integrate it into their personalities. It is a time for pride in the ability to make decisions and accept the accompanying restraints, responsibilities and consequences of those decisions. Adolescence marks the beginning of a search for meaning which will last a lifetime.

Concerns Most adolescents are concerned about such things as accurate communication, respect for their privacy, the clash between values which are "taught" and values which are "lived," keeping friends and increasing their popularity, restrictions placed on them because they are still "too young," and personal growth, especially as it pertains to getting to know themselves better. They are very protective of their own concerns. They seek to give the impression that they are "their own" people and have no need for anyone else.

Needs The needs of adolescents are usually unspoken but are very real. Probably highest on the list is the desire for acceptance. This is most obvious with respect to peers and is apparent in conformity — in hair style, dress, tastes, and the tendency to form tight cliques. But the adolescent also has a great need for acceptance and approval from adults. Adolescents need challenges and perform best when challenged in different ways and encouraged to believe that they have the ability to rise to the occasion.

Adults can help adolescents grow by giving them sincere praise and by expressing confidence, understanding and trust in their goodness and worth. It is important that adolescents have the freedom to make mistakes, but they also have a great need for adult acceptance despite their errors and awkwardness. While displaying an accepting attitude, parents and other adults should help young people correct such problems and should enforce loving discipline when necessary.

Sexuality This is a time of rapid physical growth and sexual maturing. The latter's obvious implications for personal relationships are not to be taken lightly. Today society hastens boy-girl relationships in many ways. Parents face the task — by no means easy — of striking an acceptable, understanding balance between a legitimate permissiveness and over-protectiveness.

Self

Junior high students are looking for meaning — for ideas and values by which they can become whole persons able to take their places in the adult world. They are beginning to reach out for knowledge to go beyond generalizations, to recognize personal insights, and to respect quality. They need to feel successful in communicating their ideas and concerns to their parents. Their opinions should be discussed and taken seriously. Reflection and self-analysis are important parts of adolescents' lives, for which they need quiet time.

BELIEFS AND MORAL TEACHINGS

Religion   Religious instruction on the junior high level investigates the meaning of covenant as a special love relationship with God, approaching it from both a historical and a personal perspective. Sacrifice and prayer as aspects of the Christian life of faith are emphasized. Love and service to God and man are also presented as essential elements of this life. Students are encouraged to make hope and charity part of their personal lives.

Church   In these years the Church is studied — as the Body of Christ, the Mystical Body, the sign or sacrament of Christ, and also as a people and an institution. As they study the Catholic Church as the all-embracing means of salvation in which the fullness of God's revealed truth is present, young people also learn of the many elements of holiness and truth found in other churches and religious bodies. Through a study of the Protestant Reformation and of modern Christianity, they grow in respect, understanding and appreciation of the spiritual riches of other Christian communions. At the same time, they also grow in appreciation of the uniqueness of the Catholic Church and develop a fuller understanding of ecumenism, whose ultimate goal is the unity of believers for which Christ prayed at the Last Supper: "That they all may be one." Young people should also be taught about the basic structure of the Church as established by Christ. The special role of the Holy Father and the Bishops should be explained.

Christ   Jesus Christ is studied and experienced not only as our Saviour, a historical person who won redemption for all, but also as One who lives today in the world and enables all people to respond to their special relationship to the Father arising from the life of grace which Christ revealed. Christ's law of love and its implications for community are explored further.

Mary

After Christ, Mary has the highest place in the Church. As our spiritual Mother she is uniquely close to us. Religious instruction explains her special gifts as the Mother of God — her preservation from all stain of original sin, her assumption into heaven. Special veneration of Mary should be taught by word and example. Mary gives a perfect example of obedience, humility and faith: she is a model whom all should imitate.

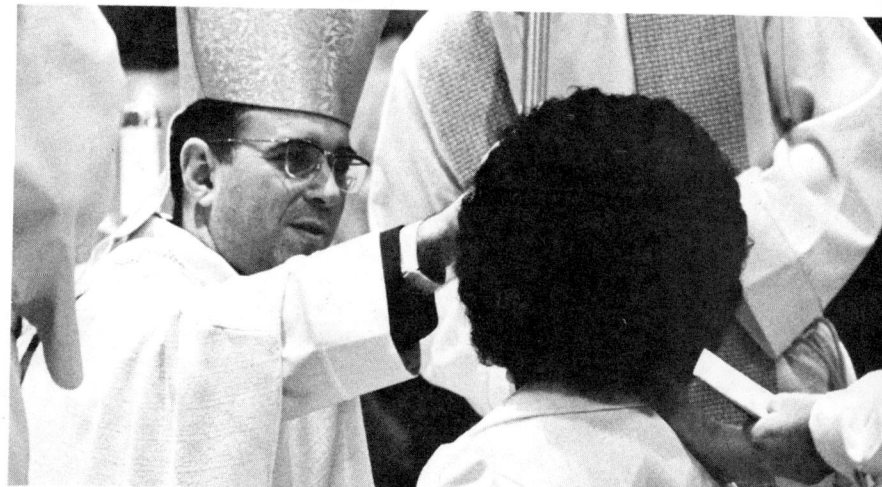

Confirmation

As the Church, in Baptism, invited the individual to accept faith, so now it extends a further invitation to the junior high student in the Sacrament of Confirmation. The word confirmation means "strengthening," so the Sacrament of Confirmation is a sacrament of strength for the person who has received the gift of faith in Baptism and has been nourished by the Eucharist. Confirmation, like Baptism and the Eucharist, is a sacrament of initiation, by which Christians more fully become the image of their Lord and are filled with the Holy Spirit.

The Holy Spirit strengthens the person confirmed and invites him or her to share the faith with others by loving service of God, the Church and other persons. At Confirmation the whole Christian community and the young person being welcomed into a

mature role in that community celebrate together the gifts of God which are the effects of the outpouring of His Spirit. Anointing and the imposing of hands are the signs of Jesus' presence and action in Confirmation.

The Beatitudes call Christians to adulthood. They ask for a personal response to Christ and to others in the Christian community. Reception of Confirmation reinforces these values at this age level. While students need not memorize the Beatitudes, they should discuss their implications for their personal lives.

The Beatitudes

1. Blessed are the poor in spirit; the reign of God is theirs.

2. Blessed are the sorrowing; they shall be consoled.

3. Blessed are the lowly; they shall inherit the land.

4. Blessed are they who hunger and thirst for holiness; they shall have their fill.

5. Blessed are they who show mercy; mercy shall be theirs.

6. Blessed are the single-hearted; they shall see God.

7. Blessed are the peacemakers; they shall be called Sons of God.

8. Blessed are those persecuted for holiness' sake; the reign of God is theirs.

It is wise to take advantage of the abounding energy and generosity of adolescents and encourage and guide them in specific service projects. These provide opportunity for both the study and the practice of the Spiritual and Corporal (or physical) Works of Mercy.

Spiritual Works of Mercy

1. Counsel the doubtful.
2. Instruct the ignorant.
3. Admonish the sinner.
4. Forgive injuries.
5. Comfort the sorrowful.
6. Bear wrongs patiently.
7. Pray for the living and the dead.

Corporal Works of Mercy

1. Feed the hungry.
2. Give drink to the thirsty.
3. Clothe the naked.
4. Shelter the homeless.
5. Visit the sick.
6. Visit the imprisoned.
7. Bury the dead.

Vocations

In Confirmation the young person is called to share his or her faith with others. It is well at this time to discuss the many ways people are serving in the Catholic community, as well as the positive responsibility all Christians have to serve the wider civic community by witnessing to their beliefs in the fields of government, business, education, science, labor and the other sectors of American life. This comes about by following Jesus' call to different vocations in life: marriage, priesthood, permanent diaconate, religious life and the single state. It is well to encourage young people to pray to the Holy Spirit to know how they can best serve. In a particular way they should be encouraged to consider the priesthood or religious life. A mini-retreat or day of recollection based on the theme of vocations is recommended.

Conscience Formation

Time should be set aside as a continuing part of the junior high program to guide young people in forming Christian consciences. They must be helped to see that God has given us a way of life which is to be followed. Each one must make the effort to learn as much as possible about this way and accept it with an open and generous heart. This means truly listening and responding to God's teaching when it is presented to us. Teenagers should have opportunities for assistance in evaluating their actions and omissions in light of Christ's message and their present responsibilities. Parents should encourage, support and assist their children in efforts to form truly Christ-like moral judgments.

Conscience is not intuition or instinct. It is a practical judgment which a person makes about whether an action which he or she is about to perform here and now is according to God's plan (good) or against that plan (evil). Conscience must be formed if its decisions are to be correct. Help in forming conscience comes from prayer, the commandments, Scripture, the teachings of the Church, the example of Jesus and the saints, and the experience of living in a good family. The teachings of the Pope and the bishops offer guidance and norms for applying the enduring values of Christian morality to the specific situations of everyday life. Young people should be taught that there are moral values which do not change and are not to be disregarded or violated by anyone in any situation.

Sin

God made people free but our freedom has been badly impaired by original sin. We are still free to choose the good but it is more difficult for us to do so. We experience many temptations which appeal to our weakness. Only the grace of God which is always offered to us can overcome our weakness and make us strong enough to live without sin. Through grace, we live in friendship with God. Our individual sins weaken or destroy our relationships with God

and neighbor. Through sin, moral evil and pain enter the world and people suffer.

Sin of any kind cannot be treated lightly. Venial sin is an obstacle to holiness. Mortal sin is a rejection of God which breaks our relationship of love with Him. In committing any mortal sin we reject God. We do not commit mortal sin accidentally or haphazardly. Religious education should teach young people the reality of sin, the kinds of sin, and the seriousness of acts which constitute mortal sins when they are willfully committed.

The main sources of personal sins are commonly called the "capital" sins; they represent excessive, distorted pursuit of otherwise good tendencies and are the chief reasons why people commit sins. Pride, lust and anger are examples. It is important, however, to teach young people that pride, sexual desire and anger are wrong only when they are excessive or in some sense perverted. For example, a reasonable degree of pride — an appreciation of one's own worth — is good; only when it is excessive does it become sinful pride.

Elective Courses

It is highly desirable to provide junior high students with a rich selection of content in addition to the basic elements of the curriculum. Special units to be considered might include some of the following topics: key themes of the Old Testament; the Prophets — then and now; the Parables; Christian hope and Christ's Resurrection; war, suffering and poverty; Paul and the Early Church; the cost of discipleship; faith, hope and love; Christian vocation; the moral virtues in the life of a teenager; how Jesus can help a teenager understand himself or herself.

PRAYER LIFE

Liturgical Prayer

To deepen spiritual life it is necessary to reinforce and build on past experiences. It is important that young people grow in their understanding and appreciation of the Mass at this time, in order to counteract the negative feelings about Mass attendance which are common among adolescents today. Frequent, meaningful small-group liturgies are encouraged; they are generally well received by young people. Home Masses are also to be encouraged, as are para-liturgical ceremonies. Young people should play an active part in planning these. They may choose contemporary musical forms, but they should also be guided to experience traditional hymns of our Catholic heritage, including simple Latin hymns. The purpose of such liturgies and para-liturgies is to provide a basis for the eventual integration of the person into the full community.

Spontaneous Prayer Interest in Scripture should be encouraged at this time, in order to enrich spontaneous prayer, personal prayer and Bible prayer services. The Psalms and Scriptural prayers such as Jesus' priestly prayer at the Last Supper can be used effectively. Prayer shared with parents is often important and meaningful for the adolescent.

Retreats Junior high students are at an age when they find it a powerful and rewarding experience to spend extended, prayerful time together as a small Christian community. Days of renewal and retreats help draw together the adolescent's knowledge about faith and provide opportunities for experiencing the spiritual value of prayer and meditation.

APPENDIX 1

The prayers below are printed here as a convenience to parents who are looking for these texts. It is not necessary that children learn them all. Ideally, the children will learn as they hear their parents and family pray together in the home or with others in church. Memorizing prayers should not become a task, with punishment imposed if the child does not learn them by a certain time. Prayers should be introduced when the child is able to understand them; the words should be ones the child can pronounce and comprehend. Thus the child will be able to make them a real part of life.

Come, Holy Spirit

Come, Holy Spirit, fill the hearts of Your faithful ones, and set them on fire with Your love.

V. Send forth Your Spirit and they shall be created,
R. And You will renew the face of the earth.

O God, You teach the hearts of the faithful by giving them the light of Your Holy Spirit. Grant to us that, by Your Spirit, we may be truly wise, and always experience the joy of Your strengthening presence. Through Christ our Lord. Amen.

Morning Offering

O Jesus, through the Immaculate heart of Mary, I offer You my prayers, works, joys and sufferings of this day, for all the intentions of Your Sacred Heart, in union with the Holy Sacrifice of the Mass throughout the world, in reparation for my sins, for the intentions of all our associates, and in particular for the intention recommended this month by the Holy Father.

Evening Prayer

Watch, O Lord, with those who wake, or watch, or weep tonight, and give Your angels and saints charge over those who sleep.
Tend Your sick ones, O Lord Christ.
Rest Your weary ones,
Bless Your dying ones,
Soothe Your suffering ones,
Pity Your afflicted ones,
Shield Your joyous ones,
And all for Your love's sake. Amen.

—*St. Augustine*

Grace Before Meals

Bless us, O Lord, and these Your gifts which we are about to receive from Your goodness, through Christ Our Lord. Amen.

Grace After Meals

We give You thanks, Almighty God, for these

and all Your blessings which we have received through Your goodness, through Christ Our Lord. Amen.

Memorare

Remember, O most gracious Virgin Mary, that never was it known that anyone who fled to your protection, implored your help, or sought your intercession was left unaided. Inspired with this confidence, we fly unto you, O Virgin of Virgins, our Mother. To you we come, before you we kneel, sinful and sorrowful. O Mother of the Word made flesh, do not despise our petitions, but in your mercy hear and answer them. Amen.

Act of Consecration
To Our Blessed Mother

My Queen, my Mother, I give myself entirely to

you, and to show my devotion to you, I consecrate to you this day my eyes, my ears, my mouth, my heart, my whole being without reserve. Wherefore, O good Mother, as I am yours, keep me, guard me as your property and possession. Amen.

Angelus

The angel of the Lord declared unto Mary.
And she conceived of the Holy Spirit.
Hail Mary, etc.
Behold the handmaid of the Lord.
Be it done unto me according to Your Word.
Hail Mary, etc.
And the Word was made flesh.
And dwelt among us.
Hail Mary, etc.
V. Pray for us, O holy Mother of God.
R. That we may be made worthy of the promises of Christ.

Let us pray:
Pour forth, we beseech You, O Lord, Your grace into our hearts, that we, to whom the incarnation of Christ Your Son was made known by the message of an angel, may by His Passion and Cross, be brought to the glory of His Resurrection. Through Christ our Lord. Amen.

Queen of Heaven

(Replaces Angelus during Easter Time)

V. Queen of heaven, rejoice, alleluia.
R. For He whom you were chosen to bear, alleluia.
V. Has risen as He said, alleluia.
V. Pray to God for us, alleluia.
R. Rejoice and be glad, Virgin Mary, alleluia.
V. For the Lord is truly risen, alleluia.

Let us pray:
   Father, You were pleased to give joy to the world through the resurrection of Your Son, our Lord Jesus Christ. Grant, we beseech You, that through the mediation of the Virgin Mary, His mother, we may come to possess the joys of life everlasting. Through the same Christ our Lord. Amen.

Peace Prayer of St. Francis

Lord, make me an instrument of Your peace;
where there is hatred, let me sow love;
where there is injury, pardon;
where there is doubt, faith;
where there is despair, hope;
where there is darkness, light;
where there is sadness, joy.

Grant that I may not so much seek to be
   consoled as to console;
to be understood, as to understand,
to be loved as to love;
for it is in giving that we receive,
it is in pardoning that we are pardoned,
and it is in dying that we are born to eternal life.

—*attributed to St. Francis*

APPENDIX 2

From time to time the Church has listed certain specific duties of Catholics. Some duties expected of Catholic Christians today include the following excerpted from *Basic Teachings for Catholic Religious Education,* published by the American bishops. (Those duties traditionally mentioned as Precepts of the Church are marked with an asterisk.)

1. To keep holy the day of the Lord's Resurrection: to worship God by participating in Mass every Sunday and Holy Day of Obligation*: to avoid those activities that would hinder renewal of soul and body, e.g., needless work and business activities, unnecessary shopping, etc.

2. To lead a sacramental life: to receive Holy Communion frequently and the Sacrament of Penance regularly —
   — minimally, to receive the Sacrament of Penance at least once a year (annual confession is obligatory only if serious sin is involved).*

— minimally, to receive Holy Communion at least once a year, between the First Sunday of Lent and Trinity Sunday.*

3. To study Catholic teaching in preparation for the Sacrament of Confirmation, to be confirmed, and then to continue to study and advance the cause of Christ.

4. To observe the marriage laws of the Church*: to give religious training (by example and word) to one's children; to use parish schools and religious education programs.

5. To strengthen and support the Church*: one's own parish community and parish priests; the worldwide Church and the Holy Father.

6. To do penance, including abstaining from meat and fasting from food on the appointed days.*

7. To join in the missionary spirit and apostolate of the Church.

(From *Basic Teachings For Catholic Religious Education,* p. 28)

APPENDIX 3

In teaching children about the Eucharist it is important to keep in mind their psychological state and their ability to understand language.

For the former reason, parents and teachers should be careful how they discuss the wine becoming the Blood of Jesus. Although this is, in fact, what happens, children often find it difficult to understand or psychologically accept this. Their fantasies can present real difficulties in drinking the Blood of Christ. It is advisable that parents and teachers stress at this early age that children are going to receive Jesus, the Bread of Life.

Concerning a child's ability to understand language, it is also advisable that terms such as substance or transubstantiation not be used at this early age, even though children are to be taught about the Eucharist in simple ways that are in harmony with the teaching of the Church as stated by Pope Paul VI in *On the Holy Eucharist:* "(T)he way Christ is made present in this Sacrament is none other than by the change of the whole substance of the bread into His Body, and of the whole substance of the wine into His Blood, and . . . this unique and truly wonderful change the Catholic Church rightly calls transubstantiation" (p. 46). At a later age, of course, the young people can and should be taught the Church's philosophical explanation for the miraculous change which occurs at Mass at the time of the consecration.